THE MIRACLE OF THE BOWL OF MILK

Prophet Muhammad for Little Hearts

by

Sakina Bint Erik

We all know that
the Qur'an is the greatest miracle
that Allah gave the
Prophet Muhammad ﷺ.
But our beloved Prophet ﷺ
performed many other miracles, too!
Allah allowed him to do many things
which would make
the Muslims' faith stronger,
and bring other people
who were not Muslims to Islam.

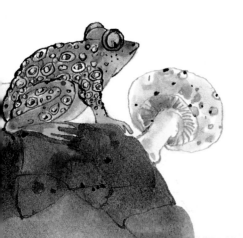

4

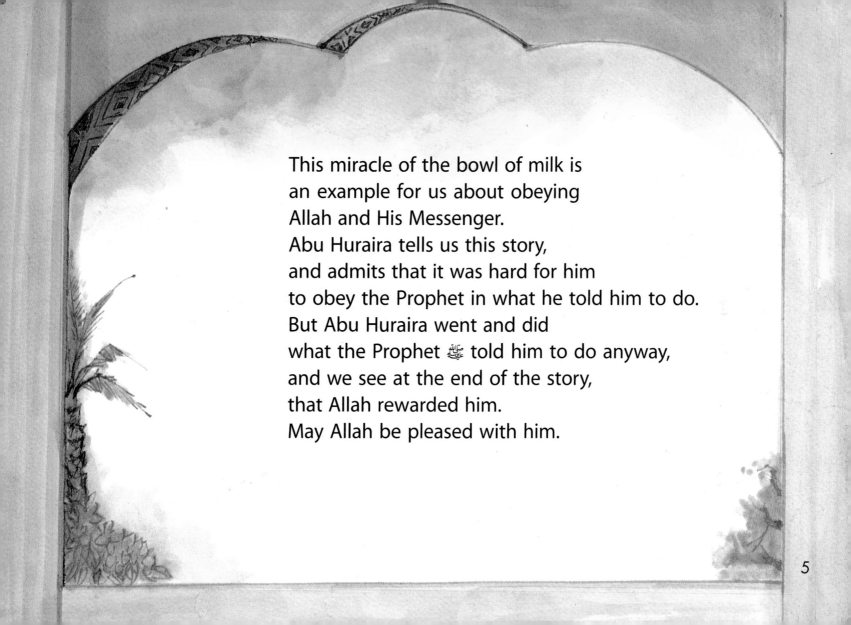

This miracle of the bowl of milk is
an example for us about obeying
Allah and His Messenger.
Abu Huraira tells us this story,
and admits that it was hard for him
to obey the Prophet in what he told him to do.
But Abu Huraira went and did
what the Prophet ﷺ told him to do anyway,
and we see at the end of the story,
that Allah rewarded him.
May Allah be pleased with him.

Abu Huraira (may Allah be pleased with him) said:
By Allah, the only One
Who is to be worshipped,
I used to be so hungry
that I had to lie
on the bare ground
to try to feel better;
I even tied a stone
to my belly sometimes
to keep from feeling hunger pains.

There was a path that
the Prophet Muhammad ﷺ
and his companions would usually take.
I sat there one day, hoping that someone would notice
how hungry I was and feed me.
When Abu Bakr (May Allah be pleased with him) came,
I asked him about some verse in the Qu'ran.
I wanted him to see how hungry I was,
and invite me as he always did.
But Allah decreed that he would talk with me
and then go on his way.
Then I saw Umar (May Allah be pleased with him),
and asked him about a verse,
but Allah decreed that he would go on his way
just like Abu Bakr.

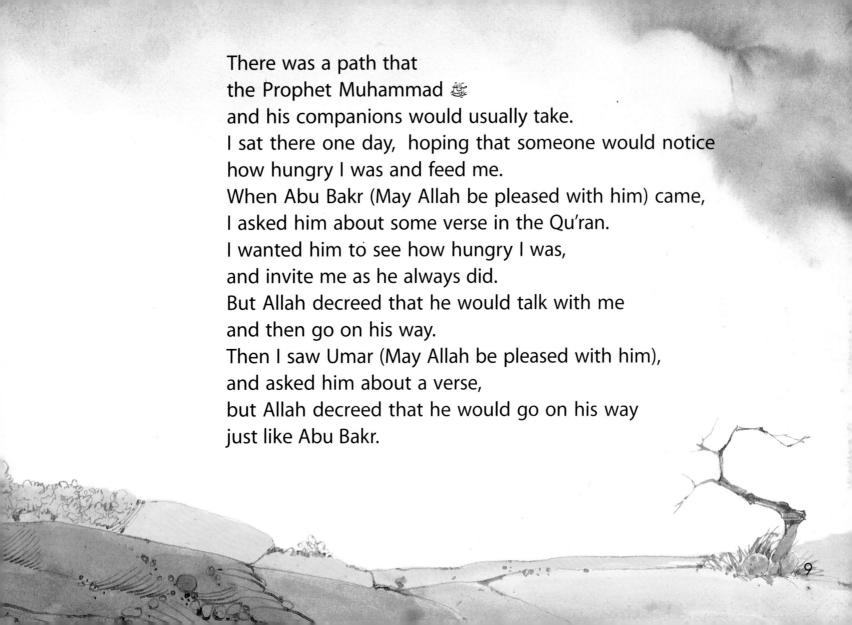

But when the Prophet ﷺ came along
and noticed me, he smiled.
He knew by the look
on my face how I was feeling.

Then he said: "Abaa Hirr !" (Abu Huraira!)

And I said, *Labbaik ya Rasool Allah!*
(At your service, O Prophet of Allah)"

He said, "Follow me."

He left and so I followed him.

We came to his home. He went in and then I asked if I could enter and I was allowed in.

The Prophet ﷺ found in his home
a bowl of milk, so he asked:
Where is this milk from? *Min aina haatha labanu?*

The people in his house replied:
Somebody gave it to you as a gift.

He said to me: "Yaa Abaa Hirr!
(Oh Abu Huraira)"

And I said, *"Labbaik ya rasool Allah!"*
(At your service O Prophet of Allah!)

And he said: "Go ask the people of
As-Suffah to come to my home."

Abu Huraira tells us
that the Ahlul Suffah
were the poorest (most *miskeen*)
Muslims; they had no family, no money,
and no one to help them.
When the Prophet ﷺ
was given charity (*sadaqa*),
he would send it to the Ahlul-Suffah
without taking anything from it.
But if the Prophet ﷺ
were given a gift (*hediyah*),
he would send them some of it
and take some for himself.

Abu Huraira continues with the story:
I wasn't happy about what
the Prophet ﷺ ordered me to do.
I thought to myself, "This milk will not be enough for all those people!"
I thought it would be better for me to get a chance
to drink from it to make myself strong.
I was so tired and hungry,
and it was only really enough for one man.
But the Prophet ﷺ of Allah had told me to give the milk to them!
I did not think any would be left for me,
but there was nothing for me to do
except obey Allah and His Messenger.

So I went to the Ahlul-Suffah
and I called them.
They came and asked permission to enter,
and they were allowed in.
They settled into seats in the house.

The Prophet ﷺ said: "Ya Abba Hirr!"

And I said, *"Labbaik, ya rasool Allah!"*

He said, "Take the milk and give it to them."

So I took the bowl and I offered it to the first man.

He drank his belly's fill
and then passed the bowl back to me.
There was milk left in the bowl,
so I gave the bowl to another man
and he drank till his belly was full,
and then passed the bowl back to me.
Still I saw milk in the bowl,
just as much as there had been
before anyone had drunk from it!

Each and every one of the people there
had their belly's fill of milk.
Then I came to the Prophet ﷺ.

He took the bowl and held it in his hand.

He looked at me and smiled.

And he said, "Abaa Hirr!"

And I said, *"Labbaik, ya rasool Allah!"*

He told me, "Now it is just you and me left."

And I said, "You have spoken the truth,
Oh Prophet of Allah."

He said to me, "Sit down and drink."

So I sat down and drank.
And he said again to me: "Drink! (Ishrab!)"

So I drank until I couldn't drink any more.
He kept urging me, "Drink! (Ishrab!)" until I
had to say: "No, by the one who sent you
with the truth, I have no room
in my belly for it!"

Then he said, "Then give it to me."

I gave him the bowl,
and he praised Allah, and said *"Bismillah,"*
and drank what was left.